The Gypsy JOURNALS

Adventures of a 62-Year-Old Orphan

Shari Lee Fleming

ISBN 978-1-63784-047-4 (paperback)
ISBN 978-1-63784-009-2 (digital)

Hawes & Jenkins Publishing
16427 N Scottsdale Road Suite 410
Scottsdale, AZ 85254
www.hawesjenkins.com

This book is dedicated to my wonderful parents, Earl and Marlene Fleming, who now reside in heaven.

To my mom, thank you for always loving me no matter how bad I was. Your complete acceptance of me gave me the confidence to always be myself and to follow my dreams. I hope you are dancing in heaven. I will love you and miss you until my last breath.

To my dad, thank you for loving me even when you didn't like me. Your strength of character and fighting spirit live on in me, and I hope I make you proud. You were the first one to ever call me Gypsy, and I will wear that title proudly into my future journeys. Thank you for being a good man. I will love you and remember you forever.

To my sister, Vicki, thank you for always being there and for being the voice of reason during the chaos. Going through the really hard times in life is so much more bearable with a sister like you. I love you, and I thank you for all that you are. I think Mom and Dad are proud of the great team that we have become!

And to God, my heavenly Father, thank You for giving me life and life in abundance. Without You, we would all be just dust in the wind.

My wonderful parents, Earl and Marlene Fleming,
on their 60th wedding anniversary

Me, Mom and my sister, Vicki, on Easter, 1960

My sister, Vicki, Mom and I at the movies, 2018

Preface

On November 20, 2020, eight days after losing my mom to Alzheimer's disease, I embarked on a journey into the desert. Here I would spend the next five months mourning her death but also remembering and rejoicing in her and her life. Traveling and exploring new places every day while finding God's handiwork and beauty along the way. Taking this journey was the most healing thing I could have done at the most devastating time in my life.

This is a story of healing, of grieving, and of exploring. Appreciating and basking in God's glorious creation. Thank you for sharing in my journey with me.

> "A journey well shared is a journey well enjoyed."
> —Unknown

Our travel trailer, Easy Breezy, in the Arizona desert

CHAPTER 1

The Beginning

November 2020

What do you do when your purpose in life is taken away? You can either (a) find another one or (b) not have one for a while. I am choosing option B. Let me tell you why.

For the last ten years (and pretty much my whole life), I have been my mother's keeper. I have followed her around the countryside with her illnesses and various surgeries. From Wisconsin to Florida and back to Wisconsin. From hysterectomy to diverticulosis to bladder sling to knee replacement to hip surgery and to what would ultimately take her life at the age of eighty-seven...Alzheimer's disease. During the last decade, Alzheimer's has slowly robbed us of our mom, but it also eventually presented us with a playful, loving three-year-old little girl! She had always been the life of the party, but now it was just her very own party! She loved to sing and dance as well as play games, puzzles, and ball. She had a killer left hook and could beat everyone at Wii bowling. Her favorite songs to sing were "You Are My Sunshine" and "Bicycle Built for Two," and she would tell almost everyone she met that she loved them.

I was so very proud of the sweet, funny, spunky girl that she had become just as you would be proud of your own child. She also had a naughty side and loved to collect things, even things that were not hers! Anything that wasn't nailed down at her care facility was fair game for Marlene the Collector, and it would all end up on her walker. Sometimes she had so much stuff piled up it would just all fall off and end up on the floor. The caregivers always kidded that when they saw her leave her room, they would say, "Uh-oh, Marlene's on the go. Look out and watch your stuff!"

I was always her daughter, but for the last ten years of her life, I also acted as her mother, her friend, and especially her advocate. I would call, email, and chase down her caregivers, nurses, administrators, and doctors to get answers and try to make sure she was being given the best care possible and that she had as much joy in her life as could be found in a care facility.

Covid really threw a wrench in the works, and sadly, my mom and her quality of life really suffered. The isolation and lack of attention allowed the disease to take over, and her decline was obvious, physically and cognitively. We were helpless to do anything about it but did keep up with Skype calls and window visits, singing with her and saying "I love you" over and over again.

She started eating less and got weaker and weaker, eventually becoming bedridden. Through her decline, however, she still sang with her daughters and caregivers and continued telling everyone, "I love you."

Our sweet Mama Marlene went to be with our Father in heaven at 1:30 a.m. on November 12, 2020. She passed away peacefully in her sleep just as her daddy had done years earlier. Even though the fact that she is no longer here with us is heartbreaking, knowing that she is in heaven, dancing and singing with the angels, brings us deep comfort and peace. We know that she is in good hands and that we no longer have to fight to make sure she is being cared for as lovingly and carefully as she deserved to be. I am no longer my mother's keeper, but I will always be her daughter and will never lose those memories of having her in my life for sixty-two wonderful years.

So, that is why my plan is to be purposely unpurposeful. The purpose of my life, or mission, if you will, especially for the last ten years, has been completed. I need a new assignment, but for now, I need to rest and have peace and joy and I need to mourn. To grieve. To remember. To exist. I want for now to have no purpose except to breathe and allow my broken heart to beat and to heal.

I know that someday, maybe soon, maybe not for a while, God will instill in me another purpose, another assignment, and I will partake in a new mission. He will know when I am ready to be a warrior again. But, until that day, I will just be...purposely unpurposeful. Thanks for stopping by, and I'll see you on the road.

"God could not be everywhere, and therefore He made mothers."
—Rudyard Kipling

"There are no goodbyes, wherever you are, you will always be in my heart."
—Mahatma Gandhi

Mom and me

CHAPTER 2

The Journey

November 2020

In Chapter 1, I talked about my mom and her unexpected death on November 12, 2020. She did not die of Covid, but the disease definitely and unfortunately caused her death to come sooner than anyone had anticipated.

Now that I am no longer my mother's keeper, I am learning to find my place in the world again. Because my mom now lives in heaven, my main purpose in life has ended, and I am waiting for God to give me a new assignment.

But until that day, I am planning to have no purpose on purpose other than to live and to breathe. To check out of society and just exist. I understand that some people will look at this as being selfish, not living up to one's potential, or giving up. I'm here to tell you that in no way, shape, or form am I giving up or throwing in the towel!

Quite the contrary—I am embracing and appreciating the opportunity to just be and to heal; to not let the could'ves, would'ves, and should'ves of my mom's death haunt me; and to not let the what-ifs of her care or lack thereof wake me up in the middle of the night and torment me anymore!

Am I glad that my mom passed away? Heck no, and what a stupid question! But I will admit that knowing she is in heaven with Jesus, dancing with my dad, and is whole, happy, and beautiful again, yes, that is a huge relief and a great blessing from God!

So now what's a sixty-two-year-old orphan to do? Did I mention that I don't have children and that my mom in her Alzheimer's had become like the three-year-old little girl that I never had? To say it's been tough would be an understatement. My focus and purpose for the last ten-plus years was to act as my mother's keeper, her helper, and her advocate, staying on top of meeting her needs and making sure her care facility was giving her good, quality care—not an easy task, especially during Covid.

But it is what it is, and I must now face facts. She is gone, and I must learn to accept that and get on with my life. I always said that as soon as my mom moved to heaven, my plan was to travel, to embrace my inner gypsy and go on a road trip across America. To hook up our little sixteen-foot trailer and go boondocking around the countryside. For those of you who aren't campers, boondocking means to camp off the grid, far from the services and chaos of RV parks and developed campgrounds. It's a more peaceful and reclusive way of camping that can land you in beautiful and rustic destinations for days or weeks at a time.

My dream is to be a nomad where my only home is on wheels and we can pick up and move whenever and wherever the urge strikes. To being free and to know that the future is wide open and that the destination is not as important as the journey to get there. To find myself, and to rejuvenate and recharge while I wait for God's next assignment.

"Not all who wander are lost."
—J. R. R. Tolkien

On November 20, eight days after my mom's journey to heaven, we loaded up our sixteen-foot Scamp camper that we call Easy Breezy and headed southwest toward Arizona, looking to explore places that we had never been before. We are currently boondocking in Easy Breezy, staying at a free area near a small town appropriately called Why, Arizona! Why not Arizona? The sun is out every day, we can stay as long as we like, and we can do as much or as little as we are motivated to do. We are living large by living small. No electricity, no heat, no running water. Just total freedom, the warmth of the sun by day and a campfire by night; enjoying the beauty of the land, existing, breathing, reflecting, healing. Awww… Life is good!

> "But in the desert, in the pure clean atmosphere,
> in the silence—there you can find yourself."
>
> —Father Dioscuros

So, for now, that is where you will find me. On the road to rediscover my purpose again and, while doing that, just being free and enjoying the ride along the way!

Until next time, thanks for checking in, and I'll see you on the road!

CHAPTER 3

Christmas

December 2020

Greetings from the high desert of Arizona! We are living under the sky in our sixteen-foot camper we call Easy Breezy. Even though it is winter, the sun is warm by day, and the campfire warm by night!

It is Christmas week, and even though everyone is getting ready for the holidays, this year is different. This year is difficult. This year is a little bit of a downer. You see, this is the first Christmas that my mom is spending in heaven. For sixty-two years, my mom has always been there for me, always ready with presents, cards, cookies, love, and lots of family traditions. So yes, for me, this year will be a bit of a bummer.

And then, of course, there is everyone else dealing with the stupid virus! Families are being told not to get together at Christmas and that if they do dare to be in the same building at the same time, to make sure that they have masks on and stay at least six feet apart—and definitely no hugging or kissing! *Say what?*

Covid is definitely the biggest grinch in the history of grinches and a much bigger Scrooge than Ebenezer himself! So yeah, to say that Christmas 2020 is different, difficult, and a bit of a downer for everyone is probably the biggest understatement of all time!

However, I am here to tell you to look on the bright side. If your loved ones are still on this side of heaven, take heart! You may be limited in being able to be with them this Christmas, but at least you still HAVE them! To give gifts to, to bake cookies for, to love on and appreciate and to laugh with or get mad at! So please, even if it's not the "norm" this year, celebrate and do it to the fullest! This, too, shall pass, and my prayer is that Christmas 2021 will be the biggest, best, and brightest Christmas ever!

If Covid has done any good in this world, I would say that it should have brought us all a newfound appreciation of life, of family, of friends, and of enjoying the simple things in this world! To recognize, prioritize and appreciate what is the #1 most important thing in life... TIME!

> "If you love life, don't waste time, for time is what
> life is made up of."
> —Bruce Lee

And that is why I have decided to be purposely unpurposeful, to slow down, to recognize and value the things of this world that God has given us all. The sun, the moon, the stars. The air that we breathe. The beauty of the sky, the land and the sea. The critters that are everywhere, as big as a bull, as small as a bee and everything in between.

I have a newfound appreciation for watching a bird peck at the sand, a dragonfly dancing in the breeze, a coyote calling in the dark, or an owl hooting at the moon. I want to never again take these things for granted or to stop being in awe of everything that God has created in this universe.

I hope that I never take my mother's love for granted even for one minute of my life. And I know that her love is still alive in me even though she is gone.

So on this day, I commit to celebrating Christmas and the real meaning of the day. It is the day that God so loved the world that He gave His one and only son, that whoever believes in Him shall not perish but have eternal life.

How can we feel that Christmas is anything but beautiful? It is a gift of the greatest sacrifice for all of us to be together in heaven with our loved ones again someday! So please, no matter what is going on in the world, remember that Jesus is the reason for the season.

Have a very Merry Christmas, and I'll see you on the road.

CHAPTER 4

After Christmas

December 2020

Well, folks, we made it through Christmas! I hate to say it like that because, as all believers know, December 25 is a very important, awesome, and amazing day. It is the miraculous birth of our Lord and Savior, Jesus Christ!

Unfortunately, society has made it all about Santa Claus. The overwhelming pressure of shopping, wrapping, baking, decorating, entertaining, and sending cards has turned the occasion into a frenzy instead of what it should be…a day to peacefully remember, reflect, and rejoice with deep awe, adoration and appreciation. To surround oneself with those you love and those who love you and just BE. Be together. To remember the birth of Jesus, who came to the earth to live and to die as a man so that we may have the gift of eternal life. To reflect on all the blessings that God has given us; and to rejoice in the blessings yet to come.

When you lose someone you love and they are no longer present during special occasions such as Christmas, it doesn't seem quite the same. Family traditions become lost, and the excitement and enjoyment of the event seem to dim. But the memories—oh, the memories—of past times, the love and comfort of family traditions, the songs that were sung, the cookies that were made, and the meals that were prepared and enjoyed together…those are the ties that bind and will sustain you throughout the rest of your years. Of course, it is necessary to make new memories with the newest additions to the family even though they will be different ones. And I'm here to tell you it's okay to be different!

So my Christmas this year, the first one without my mom, was okay. It was different. It was weird. But it was fun. I got through it. I remembered. I reflected. I rejoiced. And then I cried. I cried because I miss my mom and know that my life will never be the same without her in it. I cried because the world got a lot less colorful without her sparkle. I cried because I will never again eat one of her cookies or hear her say "I love you."

But I know that I will be okay. I know those memories made me who I am today and they will sustain me. Even though I can no longer hear her voice or feel her touch, I can still remember. I can still reflect, and I can rejoice that she was my mommy and that she loved me. What a blessing!

Next on the calendar is New Year's. I don't know about you, but I'm pretty sure most of the world is totally ready to get 2020 over and done with! To start a new year, one with a promise of better things to come.

We will be celebrating New Year's in the warm desert somewhere in our little sixteen-foot trailer we call Easy Breezy. We have no agenda, no time constraints, and no appointments other than when Mother Nature calls! Enjoying the simple things in life and taking life as it comes. Life in the slow lane. Having no purpose on purpose except to enjoy and appreciate all that God has given us. The freedom to travel to wherever the road takes us. The loyal companionship of our fellow travelers, our dogs, Rocky and Raven. The comfort and warmth of the sun, which seems to be always out in Arizona; admiring the unique beauty and mystery of the desert and its creatures. The promise and hope of a new day to enjoy on God's green earth.

And we do all this while carrying the love of our family—past, present, and future—in our hearts. The journey would never be the same without that most important ingredient. So wherever you are and whatever you are doing, please do not forget to practice the three

*R*s: *remember*, *reflect*, and *rejoice*! I promise your life will be better if you do.

> "Wherever you go, go with all your heart."
> —Confucius

Thanks for stopping by, and I'll see you on the road!

CHAPTER 5

The Letter

December 2020

It was suggested by my grief counselor today that I should write a letter to try to have "closure" about the chain of events leading to my mom's unexpected death on November 12, 2020.

I know that I am harboring a lot of anger and resentment toward her former care facility, and I believe it is *righteous* anger. Therefore, I feel I am entitled to have it. But the question is "Do I want it?" Do I want to keep that anger alive even if it's on the back burner? Is it doing me any good whatsoever, allowing myself to have it? Is it making the sudden passing of my mom any less painful?

The answers to all these questions, of course, is *no*, and that is why I am going to write it. I am going to clear the air, state the facts, and go on the record that I believe the "involuntary discharge" by the care facility that my mother was forced to undergo, sadly and without justification, took months off her life!

Before I continue, let me backtrack a little. We admitted our mom into the care facility on September 25, 2015. She was in her fifth year of Alzheimer's at that time and needed help with almost all her daily cares. During her admission, we were advised that she could live at this "memory care" facility throughout all the various stages of her disease up to and through her death. If we were not given this promise, we almost certainly would never have had her move in. We wanted and needed the assurance that this was going to be her forever home until she moved to heaven. The thought that she could live out her life there was very comforting.

Well, guess what? THEY LIED! As if living with the isolation and torment of Covid wasn't enough, on September 3, I received a phone message out of the blue from the administrator of Mom's facility stating that she needed to talk to me about mom's cares. I assumed that there might be an issue with her care or something that needed to be changed in her room or something of that nature. Boy, was I wrong!

I called the administrator back immediately, and the words she said will haunt me forever: "We can no longer provide for your mother's needs, and you have thirty days to find another place for her to live!" Needless to say, I was blindsided and just in shock almost to the point of being speechless!

I do remember asking, "What needs?" to which she responded, "Her behaviors." I then asked, "What behaviors?" and she told me of some recent events where my mom (who was then in her tenth year of Alzheimer's) had been getting into the dishes (made of glass) in the dining room and had broken some. My next question was "Can't the dishes be kept in the locked cupboards?" but I never really received an answer. Her decision was *final*, she said, and there was nothing that we could do about it! We received no notice, no warnings, no chance to talk to her doctor, nothing! Just a phone call!

I would like to state at this time that I believe the behaviors that my mom was having were totally in response to the boredom, isolation, and loneliness of not having her family there for months due to Covid.

The next thing I remember is thinking of some not-so-nice names to call her, but in my state of shock, I simply told her how coldhearted I thought she was being and that I could not understand how she could even sleep at night, treating people like this! Her response was to hang up on me.

So there I sat. Shaking. Crying. In disbelief that we now have to find another care facility that we could move our poor eighty-seven-year-old mom with Alzheimer's into during *COVID*!

Long, sad story short, we found a nice place (with what we could tell without being able to get a pre-move-in tour or visit) in another town where we believed our mom would be comfortable, happy, and well cared for, for months or possibly years to come.

It was not to be. ☹ The move was just too much of a change for her with unfamiliar rooms, hallways, and faces, especially without her loving daughters being able to be there with her for the adjustment. She could never learn where her new room was, and she began declining physically and cognitively. And then she began falling. She was given a wheelchair to use, but then sadly, she stopped eating and drinking much and started to lose weight rapidly. My sister and I tried everything we could think of: brainstorming with the kitchen about what her favorite foods are and asking if they could please offer her those if she wasn't eating; getting meal-replacement shakes for extra calories and protein, bringing her strawberry shakes, key lime pie, and Mandarin oranges. Anything and everything that would keep her from losing any more weight, anything to keep her from dying.

Sadly, even with all our efforts, it wasn't enough. Our sweet Mama Marlene passed away quietly and, we were told, peacefully during the early morning of November 12, 2020. She only made it forty-four days at her new facility. It was just too much to expect someone who was in her tenth year of Alzheimer's and forced to move out of the only home she knew to acclimate to a brand-new and unknown environment.

So did the forced eviction from her home have anything to do with her death? *You tell me!* I believe that if it didn't kill her, it most definitely took months off her life. And that is why I have anger. And it's righteous anger.

But what do I do with it? Carry it around? Dump it on someone else? Stuff it? Scream it? Try to get justice? Unfortunately, whatever I do, it will never bring my mom back.

I'm a natural-born fighter. I'm pretty sure I came out of the womb swinging or at least yelling! When I got the call that fateful day, I sprang into fight mode. I called the management of the care facility. Then I called her case manager, our ombudsman, the AARP, the Department of Aging, the Alzheimer's Association, and even the governor of Wisconsin.

Then I called the state health department and filed a formal complaint. That complaint prompted a 126-page deficiency report against the memory care along with $18,000 in fines! Both the administrator and activity director were recently fired after the report came out.

My question is "*What took so long?*" I contacted the management of the facility the day I received the phone call evicting my mom, and if they knew it was wrong then, why didn't they step up and do something immediately? The stakes were certainly high enough because what was at stake was a woman's life! My mom might still be alive had they done something and allowed us to help with the situation instead of just evicting her from her home of five years.

So yes, for now, I'm going to keep this anger on the back burner until I can find something constructive to do with it. Until I can voice this wrongful event to the facility and let them know how their actions (or lack thereof) affected our lives and shortened the life of our precious mom. She did not deserve to be discarded, and even though she's gone, I feel the need to keep fighting for her honor. It's the only thing I can do for her now.

> "We must embrace pain and burn it as fuel for our journey."
>
> —Kenji Miyazawa

Mom

CHAPTER 6

The New Year

January 1, 2021

Greetings in the new year!

Well, 2020 is over and done. It will be a year that most likely no one will ever forget. I know it will be remembered as a sad year for our family as the year that we lost our sweet mom. But it will also be remembered as the year that she was freed from the bondage of her sick and aging mind and body. The year she was given her wings and made whole and healthy, and happy again. The year that she was reunited with her husband and parents and, most importantly, it was the year that she met Jesus.

I'm reading a book called *When All That's Left of Me Is Love* (a daughter's story of letting go). It's about a woman who was able to spend the last year with her mom, who was dying of cancer. It is a beautiful book and a warm and loving tribute to her mom and her mom's death. Reading her very sad but heartwarming story is actually making me feel better because, through her story, I feel like I am able to be a part of and a witness to the beauty of my own mom's death in some way.

The family of this woman was fortunate enough to be present during her last year. The book describes in detail the steps that they took; conversations with her mom about her commitment to live while she was dying; visits from their hospice team; and ways that they were able to bring love, joy, and even fun into their mom's life.

The things that this woman did for her mom were exactly the things that I had hoped to do with mine when it was her time to die.

On this day, the first day of the new year, I sat in the Arizona desert in the warm sun, reading this story and crying. It was a cleansing cry, very healing and even more necessary. Suddenly, out of the corner of my eye, there appeared a little grey-and-white birdie—a cactus wren—flying around the nearest bush. At that exact moment, I felt my mom's presence, her spirit, if you will, and I sensed God saying this to me: "I have given your mother a new body and a new purpose. Stop worrying about how she died and take comfort in the truth that she is with me. I am now her caretaker."

The little bird fluttered around the bush, did some pecking at the ground, and then flew off to another distant bush and then another until she was out of sight. I truly felt that my mom was stopping by to pay me a brief but invaluable visit to show me that she was not only okay but was also busy again. She was busy just like she was on this earth, but this time, with even more important work…God's work.

I have also been seeing angels in the clouds, white and wispy with wings, faces, and even sometimes a halo. I believe that God has a way of sending us signs and wonders but only if we are paying attention. In my darkest moments, I may look up into the sky and see a beautiful rainbow by day or a shooting star by night. In my heart of hearts, I believe that those signs are God saying, "Everything is going to be okay."

> "Make yourself familiar with the angels and behold them frequently in spirit; for without being seen, they are present with you."
> —Saint Francis de Sales

We have moved from the Arizona desert and are boondocking at a small lake in the very southwest corner of the state. The lake is like a desert oasis, complete with palm trees and crystal clear blue water. It seems almost like a mirage surrounded by desert with a backdrop of pink-colored mountains. Across the Colorado River lies California, which, to the gypsy in me, has always had a mystical quality. When I was a teenager in the '70s, I actually moved to California with my friends to see what the attraction was. It was pretty amazing and I started working and trying to make a life there for myself. Within a year, however, I came back home to Wisconsin to attend my sister's wedding, and I never went back. I met a boy. And also, my mom needed to have surgery, so I wanted to be around for her if she needed me.

I guess I never got to fulfill my dream of making it in California, so perhaps I still have the same calling I had as a teenager: to travel and explore unknown places and to journey across America and see all the beauty and adventure this country has to offer.

Since I am now retired, I no longer have to worry about making it somewhere. I can make it anywhere as my social security is on direct deposit! The future is wide open. God has taken over as my mother's keeper, and I have total freedom to go travel and live anywhere. That's a pretty cool feeling. And I know that wherever I am, no matter how far away I roam, home will always be where the heart is, so I carry it with me. ♥

> "Home is where your Mom is."
> —Unknown

Until next time, thanks for checking in, and I'll see you on the road.

Mittry Lake near Yuma, Arizona

CHAPTER 7

The Rainy Day

"The way I see it, if you want the rainbow, you
gotta put up with the rain."
—Dolly Parton

January 2021

Today is an unusual day for us here in sunny Arizona. It is raining! We
left our tropical oasis yesterday and headed north toward Quartzsite,
Arizona. For those of you who are unfamiliar with Quartzsite (as we
were), it is a winter home and sanctuary to an amazing amount of
RVing and camping snowbirds.

Lo and behold, this week just happens to be the week of the
annual RV show held every January. This show is normally attended
by thousands, and the small town of Quartzsite is inundated with
nomads of all shapes, sizes, and colors! We chose to come back later
in the month after the madness dies down as crowds are not our
scene, especially during Covid!

But why the big attraction to Quartzsite? The number one
reason is it's cheap! Sign me up! There are thousands of govern-
ment-owned acres out here that are run by the BLM (Bureau of Land
Management). Most camping areas in the BLM allow you to dry-
camp (no hookups or amenities) for free for fourteen days. Once
your fourteen free days are up, you just move to another area and stay
there for fourteen days and so on.

Another reason it is such a popular camping area is that it is an excellent place to enjoy the desert. There's limitless open space; dark, starry skies; and no sign of civilization other than the many like-minded fellow campers nearby. These are all the natural wonders and peaceful qualities that we are attracted to as nomads.

Besides that, you can't beat the weather even though, yes, it does rain from time to time. And it may even rain so much that you have to worry about flash floods! Oh well…into each life, some rain must fall.

"The Rainy Day"
by Henry Wadsworth Longfellow:

"Be still, sad heart and cease repining
Behind the clouds is the sun still shining
Thy fate is the common fate of all
Into each life some rain must fall."

And that brings me to think of losing my mom. How am I doing in my journey to get through the grieving process? How is this sixty-two-year-old getting along as an orphan? Well, I'm getting through it. As a song by Willie Nelson would attest, it's not something you get over but something you get through. Truer words have never been spoken.

"That which does not kill us makes us stronger."
—Friedrich Nietzsche

You don't get over the loss. You survive it. You learn to live without the presence of your loved one, and you learn to do the best you can to fill the void. To remember and reflect on your life with them in it and how they have changed your world and made it a better place to be in. Not having them with you doesn't end your world. It just changes your world, and it loses some of its colors. You try to find other things to focus on to enjoy life as you now know it without them in it. This is your "new normal," whatever that over-used term means.

And I am getting through it. Slowly but surely. Baby steps. Appreciating God's wondrous creations, which are all around us! I notice little things that remind me of my mom. I look through the hundreds of old pictures, realizing even more than ever the joy that we brought into each other's lives. I am facing the hard, cruel fact that those times are over and done but finding comfort that the memories and the love will always remain. Knowing and being thankful that nothing can ever take that away.

> "It does not matter how slowly you go as long as you do not stop."
> —Confucius

Traveling to unknown places and seeing beautiful and amazing sights for the first time—this is a great way to cope and to heal along with finding joy and adventure along the way. And that is exactly what I have planned for us, our two dogs, and our little Easy Breezy camper: being on the road exploring. No agenda, no timetable, no pressure. Just being purposely unpurposeful and enjoying the path that life has put in front of us while waiting on my next assignment from God.

> "If I had a single flower for every time I think of you, I could walk forever in my garden."
> —Claudia Grandi

Thanks for joining me along the way, and I'll see you on the road!

Desert rainbow

CHAPTER 8

Welcome to Sunny California!

January 2021

We are currently camped in public lands (BLM) just below the southern entrance into Joshua Tree National Park in sunny California. It's hard to believe, but every single national park and forest in California is closed for camping due to Covid. That is a lot of campgrounds! The state has apparently been one of the most cautious ones and has been shut down for months. I always thought California was one of the less conservative states, but I must be wrong.

Anyway, we are more than happy to be camping in the BLM land, first, because it's free and, second, because it's laid-back! There are no rules or regulations and no close neighbors, just fourteen days of free camping in rugged and naturally beautiful wide-open country.

We are within a few miles of Interstate 10, which must be one of the busiest highways in America because it runs from Phoenix to Los Angeles. As I sit outside in the sun and sand, surrounded by blue skies and majestic mountains, it seems surreal to watch car after car and semi after semi traveling the interstate. All hustling and bustling to get somewhere hopefully on time. While we have all the time in the world to just be and to watch the rest of the world go by.

I feel thankful to God that I am no longer a part of that rat race: speeding to work or sitting in bumper-to-bumper traffic to get to a corporate job where everyone is trying to get ahead of the next guy or outsell or outproduce last month's quota. I put in my time and paid my dues, and now I will enjoy relishing in retirement land! Enjoying our little corner of the world wherever we may be at the moment and looking forward to the next destination.

After spending almost a week north of Quartzsite, we decided to go west into California. Our first stop after crossing the Colorado River into California was quite the surprise. It was an agricultural checkpoint looking for fruits and vegetables from other states! We had some oranges and grapefruits which we had purchased at a farm stand in Arizona so we were forced to turn them over at the checkpoint. I'm sure if they had been purchased at the grocery store, we might have been okay, but California is very strict with not allowing produce from other states to come across the border to prevent the contamination of any of their crops. It felt kind of weird. It was like they were the fruit police, and we were trying to smuggle some illegal alien fruit into the state!

We then made our way farther into the state to a place I have only heard about from one of my favorite movies: *Into the Wild*. The movie was directed by Sean Penn and is a true story about a young man whose passion is to bypass the expectations of his parents and society to go on a cross-country trip, eventually landing in Alaska. On the way, he travels as a leather tramp (slang for hitchhiker) across California and ends up getting a ride with two hippies who venture to a place called Slab City near the Salton Sea. This town is filled with loners and drifters living for free at an old US Marine base built during World War II. In 1956, everything was removed except the cement slabs (hence the name Slab City).

A few of the vets remained in the area, which eventually became a popular place for transients and snowbirds looking for a free place to stay. There is no running water, no electricity, no rent, and no property taxes in Slab City, just a bunch of eccentric souls who have rejected most of society's norms. They call the Slabs "the last free place in America" and are quite content living their lives there in squalor by utilizing everything including garbage to create makeshift housing. One would think while driving through this place and seeing what looks like destitution that the inhabitants would be miserable, but it's quite the opposite. Most live here because they are sick of worldly expectations, and they simply want to be there!

The brightest spot in the place is called Salvation Mountain, which was created by a godly man looking to spread the gospel— Leonard Knight. Leonard literally took a mountain, covered it with adobe and paint, and colorfully decorated it by painting Bible verses everywhere such as "God is love" and John 3:16: "For God so loved the world that He gave His one and only begotten son that whoever believes in Him shall have eternal life."

I believe this place resonates with me because I have always been a gypsy at heart and am always looking for the next adventure. While I am not willing to live in squalor or have a house built from garbage, I *do* want to live as simply and minimally as possible, going without the conveniences that everyone thinks they *must* have like running water or electricity. While it is wonderful to have, it certainly won't kill you if you don't have it!

And so we will continue on this journey. I am still remembering my mom and mourning her passing along the way, but being on this ongoing adventure is helping the healing process. I know that my mom would be happy for me that I am living my dream. And knowing that my mom has taken her final journey and is living in paradise, how could I be sad about that?

One final thought regarding Salvation Mountain, located at the entrance of Slab City: In the words of its creator, Leonard Knight, "Love is universal. Love God. Love one another and just keep it simple!" If we all lived like this, what a wonderful place this world would be!

Thanks for checking in, and I'll see you on the road!

Salvation Mountain, Slab City, California

CHAPTER 9

The Sunset

January 2021

Guess where we are? Yup, we are still in California! Since I last wrote in Chapter 8, we have been back and forth between California and Arizona a few times mainly because that is sometimes the only way (or the easiest way) to get from point A to point B.

It's just like our journey in life. We think we have everything figured out and know where we are headed, and all of a sudden, in the blink of an eye, along comes a giant *detour* or Road Closed sign! It is frustrating to go through these reroutes in life, but they are sometimes very necessary even if we don't know why at the time. God knows. And if we live by faith and not by fear, the journey is so very much less stressful!

> "It is good to have an end to journey toward; but
> it is the journey that matters, in the end."
> —Ernest Hemingway

Okay, now back to our travels!

The Colorado River runs along the border of Arizona and California much like how the mighty Mississippi divides the Central States. Unless you have a bridge to cross, you're out of luck! And that is why we are back in California. This time, we are on BLM land near a small town called Big River, which is right across the river from

Parker, Arizona. It's an excellent (and don't forget, free!) boondocking area filled with 360-degree views of mountains, desert, and deep-blue skies. There's also fresh air, wide-open spaces, and lots of peaceful silence (except, of course, for the noise from the never-ending traffic on the highway that brings you here). It seems that no matter how far off the beaten path you roam, there are always some signs or sounds of civilization—unfortunate in my book. I'm sure there are more remote areas, perhaps in places like Alaska, but we have no plans to explore that state any time soon. But maybe someday.

Our first sunset at this location was probably the most beautiful and colorful and the longest-lasting sunset I have ever witnessed in my sixty-two-plus years on this earth! Every few minutes, the colors would switch, the clouds would shift, and the intensity would change. I must have taken at least fifty pictures as I watched in awe and amazement such a breathtaking display of God's artwork.

To think that each and every day starts with an amazing display of color and ends with another is just mind-blowing. Usually, sunsets have a finality to them, unlike the sunrise, where the day is fresh, and new and just beginning. The opposite is true of every sunset. It is the end of the light and the beginning of the darkness.

Last night, however, I felt that God was showing me that this spectacular display was not to be looked at in a negative way as an end to the day but rather, the beginning of another adventure in our lives…the evening with all its own wondrous events: the stars and the moon, the wild animals that come out in the dark, and the stillness of the evening air. And then, of course, in twelve hours or so, we are blessed with the dawn of a new day and an opportunity to experience another day of God's beauty all over again.

Reading a message about Jesus today, I came across something that really impacted me and touched my heart. The story was about Jesus and what an amazing shepherd He was and still is today. Jesus is faithful, never abandoning us. He walks beside us our whole lives even when we do not know Him. He waits for us to come to Him, and when we do, He is tender and loving. Jesus is relentless just like a shepherd is to his flock of sheep, protecting us and pursuing us with love until our final breath.

I was not able to be there with my mom when she took her final breath. This has haunted me and continues to haunt me as my last wish for my mom was that she would die surrounded by love, hugs, and her favorite songs. It was and still is heartbreaking for me to think that she died alone.

Whenever I start feeling sad about not being there on the night that she died, I remember a conversation I had with God. It was a beautiful, warm late-summer day, and I was sitting along the lake, worrying and fretting about not being able to be with my mom at her care facility because of Covid. It was tormenting to wake up in the middle of the night and start worrying about her and wondering if she was being taken care of. At that moment on that day, as I was praying and talking to God, my spirit felt Him say, "Why are you worrying? No matter where she is, I will be there." It was so very comforting to hear this as I truly believe it was God reminding me and reassuring me that He is in control and that He is always with us no matter what is going on or no matter where we are. And I believe that no one is ever truly alone when we die because God is there, loving us and guiding us on our very last and most important journey.

Psalm 23:4 says, "Even though I walk through the valley of the shadow of death, I will fear no evil for You are with me. Your rod and Your staff, they comfort me." What a good and loving Father we have! He gives us the miracle of life when we are born, and then at the end of our lives, we are reassured by His promise of eternal life.

Life is a journey. Enjoy the ride. It's not always easy, but rest assured that God is there to help us through the rough spots of rugged roads, dark detours, and broken bridges.

> "Be brave. Take risks. Nothing can substitute experience."
> —Paulo Coelho

Thanks for checking in, and I'll see you on the road!

Sunset at Big River BLM, Big River, California

CHAPTER 10

The Death of a Camper

February 2021

On Sunday (of all days, a Super Bowl Sunday, to be exact), there was a tragedy at the public camping area in Big River, California. A camper died.

I do not know the details, nor do I need to. I just know that someone lost their life that day. One of us. One of our tribe. We campers are like a group of like-minded strangers living the same dream of exploring outdoor adventures in rural America.

This person went to sleep in their camper on Saturday night just like we all did, but when they woke up on Sunday morning, they would not live to see the end of the day. Perhaps they had plans to go to church or to make a delicious Sunday brunch and possibly watch the Super Bowl. But it was not to be. They took their last breath on this earth outside their camper that morning, surrounded by their family and friends, who must have been frantically trying to help them.

Watching as the emergency vehicles with lights blazing and sirens blaring arrived at our quiet desert sanctuary, we had no idea what was happening. The first to arrive were the fire and rescue trucks, then came the ambulance and, eventually, the sheriff's vehicles. We knew it was an emergency when they arrived, but we knew it wasn't ending well for the person when they left. The ambulance, taking what seemed like forever, and then finally leaving slowly without their lights—not a good sign. And then later, a car from the funeral home came, probably to finalize the details so the loved ones of the deceased wouldn't have to drive into town.

This event brought a solemn silence into the campground as well as a sudden greater appreciation of life. When someone loses their life, it makes your own life somehow feel even more precious. It makes you realize how short our lives are, and it invokes a thankful feeling to God for gifting us yet another day on this glorious planet.

We never know when it is our time to go. That is sometimes a blessing, but it can also be a curse. What if we don't have time to say goodbye and "I love you" to our family and friends? What if we die unexpectedly after just having a fight with our spouse or parents? What if we didn't kiss our kids and dogs goodbye when we left the house that day?

The what-ifs of life and death will drive you nuts if you let them. We must learn to have faith in God and always remember that He and He alone is in control. And ultimately, at the end of the day, we are here to live our lives and live them as fully and purposefully as possible. And at the end of our lives, whenever that may be, we can look forward to a happy and joyous reunion with our loved ones when we enter heaven along with hopefully hearing our Father's voice say, "Well done, my good and faithful servant!"

Isn't that all we really need to know about life and death? That God created us and put us on this earth for a purpose and that we must try to live up to that challenge each and every moment of our time here until our last breath?

> "I have found that if you love life, life will love you back."
> —Arthur Rubinstein

So knowing that one of our fellow campers died that day makes me sad. I am sad for them and for their family and friends. I am sad that their journey on this planet has ended. But another bigger part of me rejoices. I rejoice with the angels that this camper got to go to heaven and that his journey is now in paradise! I rejoice that this man got to spend his last day doing what he loved to do…camping in the wild blue yonder, enjoying life while surrounded by his family and friends!

What a way to go!

"Don't count the days, make the days count."
—Muhammad Ali

Thanks for stopping by, and I'll see you on the road!!

CHAPTER 11

Where Do You Wanna Be at
the End of Your Life?

February 2021

Well, we have ventured off the planned agenda (what little of one there is!) once again and have ended up in Nevada! We had no plans whatsoever to check out this state, but boy, are we glad that we did!

By recommendation of a fellow camper, we found a spectacular place to explore for a while, and of course, one of the best things about it is that it is free! Not to mention that it has bathrooms and a dumpster for our trash—two very important and very rare amenities when you are boondocking.

This amazing place is on none other than the Colorado River on Lake Mohave, which is just one of many lakes out west that were formed by damming up the river. It is called Telephone Cove, and it is exactly that: a beautiful scenic cove of white sand and crystal clear blue water surrounded by mountain bluffs. It basically looks like a tropical paradise. It's a place where you would definitely want to spend a few days and maybe even a great place to come at the end of your life.

After a few days of relaxing in the sun and kayaking, my husband came up to me to say he had seen a man who was very sickly lying on the ground under a tree. He wanted me to come over to see if I could help him. Upon walking up to this man, I could tell that he was in bad shape, and he told us that he was dying of cancer and had asked a friend to drop him off here. He had a suitcase, a couple of bottles of water, some food, a sleeping bag, and a makeshift tent with no poles! It was not a good situation for an older sickly gentleman to try to live in, let alone die in!

He proceeded to tell us that he had just been released from the hospital to go into hospice but that they were not yet ready for him to move into the care facility. So while he was waiting, this was where he wanted to be. And who could blame him? He said the doctors only gave him a few weeks to live, and this is where he and his wife used to come to camp, which, of course, gave him many wonderful memories of Telephone Cove.

We thought twice about calling an ambulance because we didn't want him to die out here on the beach while we just went about our day, but we decided against it. He seemed like he had his wits about him, and it felt wrong to *make* him go back to the same hospital he had just escaped from!

Instead, we decided to help him as there was no way the make-shift wimpy tent with no poles would protect him from the elements or keep him warm. So we rallied a few other campers together and found some poles for his tent, another tent to go over his existing tent for more rain and wind protection, an extra pillow, sleeping bags, and food. We made sure he had a walking stick to use to walk with, was taking his prescribed medications, and got some food in his stomach and a good night's sleep. We had someone checking on him multiple times throughout the night, and first thing in the morning, he was supplied with fresh coffee and a hot sandwich for breakfast.

Not only did he thank everyone for what we all did, but he also told us he felt so much better and did not think he would have made it through the night without our assistance. God knows where and when we are needed, and I feel that we were meant to be here at this campground just at this exact time.

We would have to get back on the road soon as this campground has a seven-day maximum stay, but we didn't want to leave until we knew John had a plan in place. He told us that his son would be coming here from San Diego to make arrangements for him.

It was not really our business what John would do with the limited time he had left to live, but we definitely couldn't leave until we knew that he had everything he needed to be as safe and comfortable as possible for as long as possible. So before we left, we went to the store to buy him a new tent and a cushioned pad for him to lay on under his sleeping bags. We supplied him with several days' worth of food, which should last until his kids come to pick him up.

Like I said earlier, we had absolutely *no* plans on coming into the state of Nevada, but on the way out of our previous camp, we were given this destination as a last resort. Not only is Telephone Cove the most beautiful place we have stayed so far, it also gave us an opportunity to help someone who greatly needed help. I truly believe that God directs our paths and uses us to reach out to those around us who may be in need. I'm very thankful to God that we were able to help, even in some small way.

> "Great occasions for serving God come seldom,
> but little ones surround us daily."
> —Saint Francis de Sales

Until next time, thanks for stopping by, and I'll see you on the road!

Telephone Cover near Laughlin, Nevada

CHAPTER 12

Death of a Cell Phone

February 2021

As all of us living in this modern world can attest, having a cell phone is almost as mandatory as having a car or a roof over our head. It is part of our identity, and to some, a huge part! It is an invaluable tool for communicating, paying bills, keeping track of others, and knowing what the date and time is as well as learning what is going on in the world around us.

It is also a great device to record our lives through pictures and videos. I don't know about you, but my cell phone is my one major source of connection to people and to the modern world. Imagine being out in the middle of nowhere for months at a time, and suddenly you have no way to stay connected to your friends and family, your past or your future!

"Technology is best when it brings people together."
—Matt Mullenweg

Going through the experience of my cell phone dying right before my eyes had really been a huge wake-up call. It was mainly a stark realization of my reliance on something electronic that can break, be lost, or be stolen in a moment, which is alarming to me, and I'm not sure I like it!

Many of my entire relationships are on my cell through social media. I have dozens of Facebook friends who I have never met and many people I went to high school with who are way more involved in my life than they ever were when we went to the same school together every single day! Something about that feels a little strange, but I do know that I enjoy having them in my life even if it is only via social media.

But are these kinds of relationships healthy? Do you really know someone just because you see pictures of them, their dogs, their kids, and their grandkids and learn what their likes and dislikes are by the thumbs-up or thumbs-down that they post?

I thoroughly enjoy posting all my journeys on Facebook, mostly all the fun times, but I also post most of the bad. Do my friends really know *me*, the person—like my moods and temperament and how kind or unkind I am—just by reading my posts and seeing my pictures? Would they like (or dislike) me more if we were friends in the flesh? I'm not sure. But what I *am* sure of is that when I called Verizon to tell them that my phone died and asked if I would be able to retrieve my information, especially my pictures and videos, and they said, "Probably not," *I lost it!*

My mom died on November 12, 2020 and during the months and weeks leading up to her death, I took many priceless and irreplaceable pictures and videos of her: me and her together, playing ball or doing puzzles, driving in my car, singing together, and saying "I love you" to each other. If I cannot get these memories retrieved from my dead phone, I think I will never recover! It's like her death all over again because these precious moments will never be able to happen again in this lifetime, and now I can't even relive these memories because my damn cell phone died. How could I be so stupid to rely on an electronic device to keep my memories safe and protected?

Shame on me, and shame on Verizon for selling such crappy, unreliable phones!

So here I sit, in the middle of a beautiful, peaceful location, warm and sunny on our winter adventure, and I am mourning—mourning the death of my mom and now mourning the death of my cell phone and possibly all the memories that were stored on it.

And I just start to sob, knowing that my mom is gone and dreading that now all the pictures and videos I have of her from the last weeks, months, and even years of her life could also be gone!

I feel lost and alone without a working cell phone, and that just doesn't sit well. I don't want to be this dependent on something man-made, especially something electronic made by a huge corporate conglomerate! Part of me wants to never have a cell phone ever again and go back to the old-fashioned way of communicating! But wait, is that even possible? Would that mean writing letters with pen and paper and then mailing them through the good old United States Postal Service? What a prehistoric thought! It's kind of like going back to the Dark Ages! I think we all remember the term *snail mail*? And what about phone calls, texts, or taking pictures? How is that even possible without a cell phone? The sad fact is that it is *not possible*!

This generation, like it or not, is addicted to and reliant upon modern technology. And I guess I am part of that generation because I am part of the world. I am a member of society, willing or not! I exist in this world, and I am a social creature. Therefore, I enjoy having friends, making new ones, and then staying in touch with them.

So yes, I will be taking a trip to the nearest Verizon store today against my better judgment, and no matter how wrong it will probably feel, I will most likely be buying a new and hopefully improved (and more expensive!) cell phone!

Please say a prayer that they will be able to restore my memories.

"Technology is a useful servant but a dangerous master."
—Christian Lous Lange

Thanks for stopping by, and I'll see you on the road (or maybe on Facebook!).

CHAPTER 13

The Rebirth of a Cell Phone

February 2021

Well, you guessed it. I was weak, and yes, I caved! I gave in to the pressure to be part of our modern society and got another brand-new and hopefully improved cell phone! But wait…you have to hear the rest of the story.

In the last chapter, I talked about my cell phone dying and being told by Verizon that it was quite possible that all my beloved pictures and videos would be lost. As you can imagine, that made me very, very sad, and I felt like my mom was dying all over again because my pictures, which are the last memories I have of her, were gone.

So you can understand that when the wonderful woman working at the Verizon store was able to recover all my data including my pictures, I was *ecstatic*! I was practically dancing in the aisles as it was such a relief, so much so that I did not hesitate to buy this new, improved, and more expensive phone because it now contained my precious memories.

That's not to say, however, that I didn't learn my lesson! I never, ever in a million years want to go through the trauma of thinking my pictures are lost. I am learning about the cloud as well as purchasing photo sticks to make sure that my pics are always backed up.

Boy, what a relief! Thank you, God, for having that wonderful woman at the Verizon store today! I will be forever grateful.

"It's not faith in technology. It's faith in people."
—Steve Jobs

With all this chaos happening with my cell phone, I have not talked about where we have been and what we have been up to on our adventure, so here goes…

We left our tropical cove on Lake Mohave in Nevada and ventured back into Arizona. Driving south through Kingman, we found another picturesque camping area at Burro Creek near Wikieup, Arizona. It was another site with 360-degree views of high desert, mountains, and a really cool man-made metal bridge between two mountain passes. Normally, I prefer the natural beauty over man-made stuff, but this bridge was quite spectacular!

I am pretty sure this was the very first time we actually paid for a night of camping ($6!) since November! Being the frugal (aka cheap) folks that we are, we left after the first night, found more BLM public land right down the road, and stayed there for free.

After about a week in this spot, we ventured south and found a nice BLM spot right outside the small town of Congress, Arizona. It had the feel of being in the middle of nowhere with the convenience of a small town about two miles away with all the perks: a few stores, a nice park with a bathroom, a gas station, restaurants, and a laundromat—all the amenities us boondockers enjoy from time to time that most city folk take for granted!

Another thing we did while we were in this area was to go visit the Granite Mountain Hotshots Memorial State Park outside Yarnell, Arizona. It is an amazing place to honor and remember the nineteen Granite Mountain Hotshots from Prescott, Arizona, who died fighting the Yarnell Hill fire on June 30, 2013.

Theirs is a heart-wrenching and tragic story of nineteen young heroes who were killed while trying to save lives and property. To go and hike the almost eight-mile round-trip trail in the mountains, which ends at their fatality site, is an overwhelmingly solemn but necessary experience. I believe it is necessary to honor their memory and to pay our respects by walking the same path that they did on that tragic day. The difference, however, is that it was not ninety-plus degrees, and we were not carrying the up-to-seventy pounds of fire-fighting gear on our backs. Nor was it up to us to try to put out a devastating forest fire!

This memorial park is the newest state park in Arizona and is a beautiful remembrance of how these heroes lost their lives in the line of duty, trying to save others. I believe that we all need to appreciate the people in this world who are on the front lines, risking life and limb to protect others.

Along our journey, we have met some pretty unique people, and this place was no exception. I met a lady while doing my laundry in the small town of Congress, and we got to talking about addiction. Turns out we are both former alcoholics. She was also a meth addict and prostitute in her past and ended up serving a few years in state prison. You never know by looking at someone where they have been in their lives or what they have been through.

Every single person alive has had trials and hardships, and we all need grace and forgiveness from God, from ourselves, and from others. She was the sweetest lady, full of life and kindness. You would never have guessed what terrible things had happened in her past. I have also had many terrible things happen to me, and I have done many terrible things to others. But I know that God has changed me, forgiven me, and given me a second chance to live a good, clean life. I try to thank Him every single day for His grace and forgiveness.

In the meantime, thanks for stopping by, and I'll see you on the road!

Burro Creek Bridge near Wikieup, Arizona

The 19 Granite Mountain Hotshots we lost were from a team within the Prescott Fire Department whose mission was to fight wildfires and when not so engaged in work to reduce growth of fire-prone vegetation. Originally founded in 2002 as a fuels mitigation crew, they were later formed as Crew 7, a Type II hand-crew in 2004, and eventually transitioned into a Type I Interagency hotshot crew in 2008.

In memory of the Granite Mountain Hot Shots from Prescott, Arizona

CHAPTER 14

The Superstition Mountains and Birthdays in a Cactus Forest

March 2021

After leaving Congress, Arizona, we ventured southeast to a place called Tortilla Flat in the Superstition Wilderness, which is in the middle of the Superstition Mountains. This place is actually a town with a population of six—seriously! It even has a post office, a bar, a restaurant, shops, a museum, and an ice-cream parlor all rolled up into one tiny block in the mountains.

We found a perfect remote spot to camp (for free, of course!) high atop a bluff overlooking a mini Grand Canyon. It was gorgeous, peaceful, and private except for the dozens of people driving out daily to the Fish Creek Hill overlook with, you guessed it, killer views of the stupendous Superstition Mountains, the highest of them coming in at an elevation of 6,300 feet.

My husband's family has been visiting these mountains and the nearby Fish Creek Canyon for several decades, so he was pretty excited to hike down to the creek. I stayed at the overlook with the dogs and ended up having a conversation with a really lovely woman. She had a gorgeous yellow Lab with her, so we bonded over our dogs, only to find out that her best friend's name is the same as mine (and spelled the same: Shari) and that her best friend's mom's name is Marlene (same as my mom)! I took that as a "God-incidence," which is like a coincidence, only it is arranged by God.

I truly believe that everything happens for a reason and that God directs our paths.

"A friend may be waiting behind a stranger's face."
—Maya Angelou

A few miles from Tortilla Flat is an amazingly beautiful mountain lake appropriately named Canyon Lake. It is another one of those surprises that Arizona has up its sleeve, and as you round a mountain pass and come upon this magical place, it is stunning. It just never ceases to amaze me how many natural wonders there are in America, especially in Arizona. Okay, this one is actually a man-made creation by building a dam on the Salt River, but still, it is a spectacular sight to see!

We do not consider ourselves to be on vacation and are therefore not tourists, so we do not usually frequent the tourist attractions. We made an exception and spent a few hours doing touristy things like shopping, visiting the ice-cream parlor, and taking our picture with the local cowboy at Tortilla Flat. It was nice but very busy and even more expensive, so we were happy to get out of there to head back to our remote and private camping spot.

After five or six days, we were short on water and supplies, so we ventured south toward Tucson and ended up at a place called Cactus Forest Campground (more BLM land), which is near Marana, Arizona. And it is exactly as the name suggests—a forest filled with cacti. I had never in my life seen so many shapes, sizes, and variations of cactus. They are beautiful and unique but painful if touched. We quickly found out (as did our dogs) that the suggestive name of the teddy bear cactus does not mean it is cuddly! It's quite the opposite as those needles are the worst we (or our dogs) have encountered thus far! Ouch!

Other than that, the place was beautiful and peaceful with a few other campers hidden in the cacti. The sunsets were amazing as there is something really beautiful about a turquoise sky, orange clouds, and big green cacti.

Both my husband and I got to celebrate our birthdays in the cactus forest as mine is on the fifteenth of March while his is on the seventeenth. We got to take advantage of a free breakfast at the local Denny's, and boy, was it good. First of all, I am usually the chief cook and bottle washer, so it was a nice treat to just sit down and be waited on for a change. And then, of course, it was free, which is our favorite part, and it was yummy to boot!

I had never celebrated a birthday in the desert before, so it was a unique experience. It was also my first birthday without my mom, which is very sad as she was always the best at making me feel special on my special day, really any day but especially on the day that I was born. So I got to experience two firsts that day—one joyful and one sad.

I know that she is watching over me and she always will be. But there is still a feeling that something is missing, and that feeling will probably never go away.

Thanks for stopping by, and I'll see you on the road.

Canyon Lake near Apache Junction, Arizona

CHAPTER 15

Apache Leap, Superior, Arizona

March 2021

After celebrating our birthdays in a forest of cacti as well as experiencing a few too many cactus attacks, we decided to venture to BLM land south of Superior, Arizona. The drive there was outstanding through some really cool towns going north along Highway 77 like Oracle, Mammoth, Dudleyville, Winkelman, and Christmas. We then traveled west on Highway 60 through Globe, Miami, and Top-of-the-World, Arizona. Come on…how can you go wrong living in a town called Top-of-the-World in Arizona?

We then explored Oak Flat Campground, which is part of the Tonto National Forest. This campground is located on Apache sacred burial grounds, and it was going to be closed to the public to allow the Native Americans to perform their ceremonies in private. Very interesting.

Another issue with this campground is that there may be plans to close it to allow a mine to be developed there. That would be very sad, especially for the Apaches, who have their sacred land there. It's just another sad example of humans raping and pillaging land for monetary gain. We need our federal land to be protected from these large corporations who are only looking out for the almighty dollar!

Okay, enough venting about that! We then journeyed into the town of Superior and found another great (and free!) BLM camping area with beautiful mountain views and wide-open spaces.

Overlooking our site was a mountain called Apache Leap. According to legend, Apache Leap is the site of a mass suicide of Apache warriors sometime during the early 1870s. The US cavalry attacked a group of Apaches, and according to legend, rather than be captured, they chose instead to leap to their deaths. What a tragic and sad event that happened at this very beautiful place.

Highway 60 going west from Globe is an amazing journey of high mountains, rugged rock, a really cool bridge, and even a tunnel carved through a mountain. It's well worth the drive, as is most of Arizona!

Around this time, I started noticing small little blossoms on the ground and new growth on the cacti. I've been told that it is a drought year and that the desert bloom may therefore not be as vibrant as usual. Well, if you look closely, you will see new life and new life in abundance! My new and improved cell phone has a killer zoom feature, and I am now obsessed with taking pictures of any kind of flower or plant. It is amazing, and I have captured many of God's beautiful creations with my camera.

"If a flower can flourish in the desert, you can flourish anywhere."
—Matshona Dhliwayo

I think about my mom and how much she loved flowers. Her birthday was May 2, and since May 1 is May Day, she would always have us make May baskets with flowers to deliver to our neighbors. That also just now reminds me of how I loved to pick flowers for my mom when I was little. Well, one spring day, I went to the neighbors, picked every single one of their tulips from their garden, and brought them home to my mom! Needless to say, she wasn't too happy when she found out where I had picked them from and made me go back to the neighbor's to apologize. Hey, what's a girl to do? I wanted to give my mommy something pretty!

So for now, I am not picking flowers, just snapping lots and lots of great pictures!

Well, folks, that's it for now. Thanks for stopping by, and I'll see you on the road.

Bridge on Highway 60 near Top-of-the-World, Arizona

Cactus flower

CHAPTER 16

Family Visits

March 2021

We decided to spend our last week in Arizona back in the Superstition Mountains, near Tortilla Flat and Fish Creek Hill. It is one of our favorite places that we have found on our adventure. We call our camping spot the mini Grand Canyon as it seems—to us at least—to be a miniature version of the real deal.

Another reason to be here is that it is the closest dispersed camping area to my husband's family: his sister in Mesa. His other sister was also visiting here, so we made several plans to get together.

One day involved a trip to Apache Junction and lunch at an old local saloon called the Hitching Post. We had a grand time eating and walking around the grounds, which is like a miniature old Western town. We took lots of pictures to remember this for years to come. Another visit involved having them out to our campsite to hang out, and then we took a drive up to the Fish Creek Hill overlook, which is a family favorite. Our last visit with his sisters before we leave to head north will involve us meeting up at Tortilla Flat for food, live music, and maybe some prickly-pear sorbet! *Yum!*

I have been feeling a little extra emotional as our winter adventure draws to a close. In a way, I wish it would never end, but then again, I am looking forward to getting "home" and back to the creature comforts of our house—things like a couch, running water, running *hot* water, electricity, a toilet that actually flushes, and a queen-size bed! Part of me feels guilty for wanting these things; it's like I have failed my nomad test! All the full-timers that I have met and who are my inspiration would probably be disappointed in me!

So, what I have decided is that it is okay to want and need to be comfortable. It's okay to want electricity, a flush toilet, or a hot shower from time to time! That does not make you a failure just because you desire these modern conveniences. You may not need them every day, but they are a once-in-awhile luxury that we have earned.

I believe I would still make an excellent nomad. To be homeless and live a meaningful and simple but FULL life with as little possessions as possible but with some creature comforts of home. To be fully engaged in your natural surroundings instead of things of the world. To be one with nature and feel closer to God. To listen more, talk less. To embrace life and to live it to the fullest. To wait on my next assignment from God where I will know that He has a new purpose for me. To continue to remember my Mom and to feel her presence as well as the presence of my other loved ones in heaven. To be aware of my surroundings; and to be open to and watchful of God's signs and wonders—that sounds like the perfect life, and I will continue my journey to get there.

I hope you have enjoyed coming along with me on this adventure. I know that it has made the experience even more valuable and meaningful by bringing you along! My hope and prayer is that every single one of you reading this will find your own special journey. The only advice I have for you is to not wait for everything to be "perfect" in your world before you decide to take your adventure. Do it whenever the opportunity strikes and do it without fear.

> "Don't wait. The time will never be just right."
> —Napoleon Hill

Keep God in the decision-making process, and He will guide you. Always be true to yourself and do not let the things of the world or other people's opinions (and believe me, they will have them!) detour you from what you want!

"Don't let the noise of others' opinions drown out your own inner voice."

—Steve Jobs

Thank you so much for traveling with me, and I'll see you on the road!

Tortilla Flat in Superstition Mountains Arizona

Near Fish Creek Hill in the Superstitions in Arizona

CHAPTER 17

Saying Goodbye to the Desert

March 2021

As I sit here, overlooking the canyon and its desert, where we have been camping for ten days, I am reflecting on the last four and a half months. We left Wisconsin on November 20—eight days after my mom took her journey to heaven. I have had a lot of time in the quiet and peacefulness of the desert to think about her and remember our life together.

Part of me is sad to leave this place as I feel I am saying goodbye to yet another part of her while celebrating and remembering her but also mourning the fact that she is gone. I believe I have moved forward in the grieving process, but I'm not ready to stop. I'm not ready to go back to Wisconsin and get back to my "normal" life. In my heart, I know that nothing ever goes back to normal after you lose a loved one. You just find a new normal and a way to get through it.

It is getting hot in the desert and will be almost one hundred degrees here in a few days. We are moving north to a higher elevation and are planning our next stop at Payson, Arizona, where the temps are in the seventies and the forest is full of big ponderosa pine trees. It is only about one hundred miles away from our current location, which just goes to show you how diverse this state is. Less than a few hours' drive will give you a totally different climate with vastly different terrain, vegetation, and wildlife.

A few days ago, we had an unexpected visitor at our camp-site…a five-day-old baby bunny rabbit! My fifteen-and-a-half-year-old dog Rocky brought it to me in his mouth and gently dropped it at my feet! It was already dark out, so I put the little guy back in the grass under a tree since I knew there was no way I was going to be able to find the nest. I was hoping that the mommy bunny rabbit would find him and bring him back to his brothers and sisters in the nest. Sadly, that did not happen, but I was very thankful that he was still alive when I found him the next morning.

So now what was I going to do with him? After learning that cow's milk is the absolute worst thing to feed a baby bunny and knowing that he wouldn't make it without eating, I spent the next couple of hours searching the internet for wildlife rescue. Eventually, I was able to reach an amazing young woman who owns and runs an animal sanctuary smack-dab in the middle of Mesa, Arizona! I came to find out she rescues all kinds of wild animals and that most of them remain living there on her beautiful two-acre property.

I was so thrilled to find a place to take Billie (yes, I named the baby bunny as I had become quite enamored with him!) not only to save his life but also to give him a good, comfortable life for the rest of his life. Crystal, the woman who owns the sanctuary, is just the kindest, sweetest person; and I could just tell that she put her whole heart and soul into this place and the animals that she's saving. Her sanctuary is a not-for-profit, which runs strictly on donations, so I was honored to be able to give her a check for $200. I was able to jus-tify this expense since upon arriving in Arizona around December 1, we have only paid for one night of camping, and that was a mere $6!

It is a wonderful feeling, being able to save a life, especially a little innocent critter's. Too many animals are hurt or injured due to mankind taking over their territory. They were there first, and we need to respect that and work *with* them instead of against them!

"Having respect for animals makes us better humans."

—Jane Goodall

Feeling confident that baby bunny Billie had a good home and was going to make it, we were able to depart from our desert home and head north to the "high country" of Payson, Arizona. The drive up there was absolutely breathtaking, and I'm sure I took over three hundred pictures during the trip.

Along the way, we were able to stop at a beautiful mountain lake fed by the Salt River called Saguaro Lake. The dogs were able to take a cool dip in the water, and we walked along the sandy beach in awe and amazement of such beauty. This place will definitely be on our wish list to return to perhaps next winter.

Arriving into Payson, we stopped for gas, water, and propane for our camper and a drive-through snack for us; and then off we went into the wild blue yonder! We were to travel north from town into the Tonto National Forest, which is full of huge ponderosa pines. The fresh air, blue skies, and sunshine made it a perfect adventure.

We found a dispersed camping area in the Verde Glen Campground. It is located on Verde Creek, but unfortunately, it was dry, as were most of the creeks we have found in Arizona. Hopefully, the snowmelt in the mountains near Flagstaff will fill these creeks in the next month or so. If not, it is going to sadly be another drought year for Arizona.

We were so far north we could even see the Mogollon (pronounced mug-e-on) Rim, which is an amazing ridge of centuries-old rock running east and west across the entire state of Arizona. Its elevation is between seven thousand and eight thousand feet. The view from the top is amazing, but we were not able to get up there due to the forest roads being closed for winter!

After setting up camp, we stopped, looked up a nearby ridge, and saw an entire herd of elk run by! *Wow!* I felt like we were in Montana instead of central Arizona. With the change of elevation, terrain, and vegetation also comes a change in wildlife. It was just another amazing feature of Arizona. You just never know what you will find around almost every turn!

Tomorrow is Easter Sunday. So after attending church, we will be heading north again, this time to a dispersed national forest area south of Sedona. I have made plans to stop by and hang out with a friend I met twelve years ago when I briefly lived in Pagosa Springs, Colorado. We both have new husbands (she was widowed), so it will be interesting to meet them and catch up. It's always great to see old friends as well as make new ones.

Until next time, thanks for stopping by, and I'll see you on the road.

Billie the Bunny

Saguaro Lake in Arizona

Verde Glen Campground near Payson, Arizona

CHAPTER 18

Cottonwood and Sedona: Visiting Old and New Friends

April 2021

After three days in the beautiful ponderosa forest near Payson, we ventured northwest toward Cottonwood. Along the highway, which was as picturesque as ever, we actually came upon snow piled along the north side of the road. I was so surprised to see snow there as the temps in that area had been in the seventies. That just goes to show you how much snow there must have been this winter to not have all melted by now, especially with all the sun and warm weather.

We drove north of Cottonwood on Highway 89A toward the gorgeous red rock of Sedona, and after a good amount of searching and traveling on some treacherous roads, we found a perfect spot to park Easy Breezy: an open space with killer views of the famous red rock formations of Sedona along with a few trees for much-needed shade for the dogs. With the temps heading close to ninety degrees and the sun moving higher and higher in the sky, my dogs have been retreating into shadier areas. I'm always looking out for my dogs (as all pet parents should!), and I am always aware of the amount of water, shade, and comfort that is available to them.

The first day at camp was spent just soaking in the views. The contrast of the red rock against turquoise sky and the green junipers was picture-perfect. Sedona is known for its healing properties, out-standing red rock formations, and deep canyons. All I know is that the beauty and wonder of God's creation is literally everywhere here! In any direction you look, beauty *abounds*!

I found out that a woman I had befriended on our journey was camping in the area. She is a full-time nomad, and she and her husband had been living in their RV for fifteen years! Sadly, tragedy struck their camp three weeks ago when her husband had a massive heart attack and died in their RV! I cannot even imagine how she must have felt at that time and how lost she must feel now. I have stayed in touch with her, but I wanted to visit with her in person so I could give her a hug and see firsthand how she was doing.

She had put her 31-foot RV in storage as she did not feel confident to drive it by herself, especially with her SUV being towed behind. So what she did was to gut out her Honda SUV and had a bed specially made to fit, which gave her a comfy place to sleep as well as lots of storage room underneath. She was traveling with her twenty-year-old kitty named Puder, so I am glad that she is not alone. She still has a lot of thinking and praying to do about her future plans, but for now, at least, she seemed confident and secure to stay in her SUV.

I don't know how well I would do if I were ever in her situation, but I do know that I have always been very independent and capable. Therefore, I believe I could definitely be a solo nomad along with my dogs and a good network of like-minded people to be connected with, especially strong, independent women like the ones I have met on this adventure.

Later that day, we drove to Cottonwood, which is about fifteen miles from our campsite, so I could reconnect with my friend Joyce, who I met while living in Pagosa Springs, Colorado, twelve years ago. We were able to visit her and her new husband in their lovely, very comfortable home and had a nice conversation over lunch. The dogs were happy to come along and lay on the cool cement in the shade on their back patio.

It is amazing to me how you can go twelve years without seeing someone and then immediately reconnect as if you were never apart! That was how it was for me with Joyce, and I am so very happy that we were able to catch up, if only for a few hours. She will definitely be someone who I intend to see every time I am in Arizona.

> "True friends are never apart. Maybe in distance but never in heart."
> —Helen Keller

Today is a rest day before we head farther north, this time to Flagstaff to get our brakes done after we find another awesome place to camp (which I know that we will!).

I received a text from my sister wanting to set a date for our mom's celebration of life this summer. Since Mom died in November in the middle of the Covid crisis, we have decided to wait until things settle down so that we can hopefully have a mask-free service, especially since it seems that almost everyone is getting vaccinated. We set the date for August 7, which is exactly four months from today. This will give us plenty of time to prepare everything once I get home. I even called the restaurant where we are planning to have the dinner after the service to make tentative reservations. I have always been a "get 'er done" girl!

While I was doing this, however, a sense of sadness came over me as this again felt like an ending. Once we have our mom's service and everyone is able to pay their respects, that's it. The ordeal is over, and now all we can do is remember her. The sense of finality makes me sad as if not having her service yet is keeping her alive in some small way. I know that these feelings are normal and are part of the grieving process. But knowing that doesn't make it any easier!

So, for now, I will keep on keeping on and we will continue our slow return trip home. Baby steps. One day at a time. One mile at a time. Returning to the "new normal" of life, whatever that may be.

In the meantime, thanks for stopping by, and I'll see you on the road.

Red rocks of Sedona, Arizona

Highway 89A north of Sedona, Arizona

CHAPTER 19

Flagstaff and Southern Utah

April 2021

We left our spot near Sedona and headed north toward Flagstaff. We are all about driving the most remote roads possible and avoiding interstates when at all possible. Well, given the few options to get to Flagstaff, we choose Highway 89A, which goes directly through the city of Sedona. Normally, it's not a big deal, but for those of you familiar with Sedona, it is a *very* popular place. Well, let me tell you it was a *zoo*! People were everywhere, driving, walking, biking...coming out of the woodwork! It took us two and a half hours to drive the forty-four miles from our site south of town to Flagstaff. However, once we made it out of the city limits, Highway 89A and its beauty were well worth the traffic jam! The gorgeous scenery of mountain passes and pine trees with glimpses of the beautiful Oak Creek made for a spectacular drive.

As expected, I found an amazing and free spot just north of Flagstaff near the Sunset Crater Volcano National Monument. It is a landmark volcano that last erupted around the year 1085! We didn't get to visit the park as we were only staying one night, but we got to see the scenic vistas and black composite soil left behind by the volcano almost one thousand years ago!

In the morning, after an alfresco coffee and breakfast in the cool mountain air, we were off to Utah. And boy, were we in for an unexpected and amazing treat!

We decided to drive through the Navajo Indian Reservation, which I thought I had driven through before and thought it would be boring, but I was *wrong*! Going northeast on Highway 160 and then north on Highway 163 takes you directly into Utah by way of Monument Valley. This valley is one of the most majestic and most photographed places on earth! This great valley consists of sandstone masterpieces that tower between four hundred and one thousand feet. The shapes, the sizes, and the colors of these gorgeous formations along with the colors of the sky and the earth make a trip through this valley an unforgettable, spellbinding experience. God was overflowing in His creativity when He formed this place!

Monument Valley is famous for its beauty and mysterious buttes and sandstone formations with the highway cut right through the center of it all. It has been the location of many famous movies such as *Easy Rider* (1969), *Thelma & Louise* (1991), and even *Forrest Gump* (1994) as well as dozens of Westerns. Driving through this place is a must-do for anyone living in this country as it is an experience you won't likely forget any time soon!

After driving north into Utah, we came into the little town of Mexican Hat, which is on the San Juan River—very scenic between the contrasting red rock and turquoise-blue river. I found the most amazing and free BLM camping area, this one at Mexican Hat Rock, which is probably the most unique rock formation we have seen yet. It is a sixty-foot-wide rock sitting on top of a much smaller rock, giving it the look of a Mexican sombrero. It is possible to climb to the top (which we did not do), where you can see the Valley of the Gods and Monument Valley. Our camping spot was directly under the Mexican Hat Rock and overlooked the beautiful San Juan River—unbelievably gorgeous, private, and yes, free!

Next on the journey was Moab, Utah, just south of Arches National Park. The park was packed, so we bypassed that (will put on our wish list for next year!) and camped at a spot on some BLM land north of the park. Moab was beautiful with Utah's famous red rock, and I am sure Arches National Park, with all its red rock vista and 2,500 stone arches, is a sight to see!

We have had the pleasure of experiencing awesome amounts of amazing beauty. I know there is so much more out there that it might take the rest of our lifetimes to see it all, but I intend to try!

Until next time, thanks for stopping by, and I'll see you on the road.

Humphreys Peak, Flagstaff. Arizona

Highway 163 leading into Monument Valley, Arizona

San Juan River at Mexican Hat BLM in Utah

Mexican Hat Rock in Mexican Hat, Utah

CHAPTER 20

Colorado: Back to Snow Country

April 2021

When I first started planning our return trip home, I wanted to go north through Wyoming and the Dakotas as I assumed it would be late enough in April to be warm in that area. Well, I assumed wrong. Not only was it not warm up there, but they were expecting snow, especially in Wyoming.

Therefore, we decided (oh, the horror!) to go on the interstate, specifically I-70, to get outa Dodge fast! But then in order to avoid driving anywhere near a huge city (like Denver), we went north through, of all places, Steamboat Springs, Colorado. For those of you who don't know Colorado, Steamboat Springs is a very popular snow skiing area with, you guessed it, lots and lots of the cold white stuff! So now we were breaking two rules of the road: no interstates and no snow!

Luckily, it was not snowing at the time we were traveling through, but there was no way we were going to be able to camp anywhere near this area as it looked like the forest roads had not been plowed for months! But it sure was pretty, and being from Wisconsin, yes, snow is beautiful as long as you don't have to go move it or drive in it!

After making it through Steamboat Springs, we drove northeast for a few more hours and eventually settled somewhere north of Walden, Colorado. We found a beautiful free camping spot by a gorgeous lake surrounded by snow-capped mountains. How majestic mountains look when the tops are covered in snow.

Now we were about to experience our coldest night ever in Easy Breezy, our Scamp camper…a frigid eighteen degrees (remember, we have no heat!). I don't know if it was the extra blanket or the extra body heat of my two dogs (or a combination of the two), but we survived the night with no frostbitten fingers or toes! The morning air was still pretty crisp, so we got an early start. Then out of the corner of my eye, I spotted six pronghorn antelopes on top of a ridge. They froze in place for a minute or two, so I was able to get my cell phone out in time to get a video of them. Then in a flash, they bounded away across the field. God sure does make incredible creatures, and those antelopes are surely one of the coolest!

So even though it was well below freezing and we were traveling through snow country, it was definitely worth it to see all this beauty and to experience these wild creatures.

Thanks for coming along, and, until next time, I'll see you on the road.

Walden, Colorado

CHAPTER 21

Nebraska and Iowa: The Great Plains and Cattle Country

April 2021

We made our way north out of Colorado and into Wyoming. Due to the cold snap, I decided to just drive through the corner of the state and get into Nebraska as quickly as possible. So yes, we got back on the interstate, and this time it was I-80. We drove east into Nebraska to the small town of Ogallala, where I had found a free camping spot at the Clear Creek Waterfowl area.

On the way to our spot, we stopped at a historical park called Ash Hollow State Park, which was a major stopover on the Oregon Trail in the mid-1850s. Ruts etched by westbound wagons were still visible on the bluffs. We don't normally stop at historical parks, but the older I get the more I seem to enjoy and appreciate history. It is a beautiful park with a very interesting place in history, so I am glad that we were able to spend a few hours there.

Right before arriving at Clear Creek, where we would be camping, I happened to notice a fenced-in area where there were a few dozen calves. Directly on the road ahead of us, one stray calf was running down the road on the wrong side of the fence. I told my husband to stop and decided to try to herd this stray calf back to the safety of the fenced-in pasture.

Because I didn't want him to run headfirst into the barbed wire, I walked past him and then, with my arms spread wide open, was eventually able to get him to the gate, which, luckily, was unlocked; and he ran safely into the company of his brothers and sisters!

Another life was saved! I don't know if he was in great danger, being away from the herd, but I didn't want to just drive by and do nothing. I was able to locate the farmer who owned the cattle the next day to let him know about the rescued calf, and he thanked me. But it seemed like it certainly wasn't the first time one of those young bucks escaped!

> "I'm not into animal rights. I'm only into animal welfare and health."
> —Betty White

After a night on the creek, we departed for our next camp, this one at a place called Streeter Park—a city park in the small town of Aurora, Nebraska. Turns out that the state of Nebraska has several city parks that offer free camping with electricity, water, bathrooms, and garbage bins at no additional charge! That's *crazy*! After boondocking in the desert and mountains for almost five months, this place was like a country club! They do accept donations, which we were happy to make for the two nights, and they also ask that you shop in their town for your needs during your stay in their park.

So we were able to spend not one but two nights with electricity (and, therefore, heat!), water, heated bathrooms with flush toilets, and garbage bins along with also being in a beautiful park with walking paths and natural beauty.

Next stop…Iowa, where we would settle for one night at Jones Creek Pond, near Moorhead. It's a cute little lake with free camping. It's hard to complain when it's free! Of course, the further north we go the colder the temps, but we are making our way back home to Wisconsin slowly but surely. There is no rush as no one is waiting for me when I get home. My mom now lives in heaven, so there is no longer any sense of urgency to rush home to see her. The closer I get to Wisconsin the more I feel the emptiness settling in, and my emotions are mixed about returning home to the new normal that will have to be established.

But life goes on, and we will all experience loss at one time or another. It's just part of the journey of life. Death is the last stop, but with our faith in God, it is the stepping stone to eternal life with Jesus. That makes death definitely a joyous occasion instead of a sad one.

"The journey of life is not meant to be feared and planned, it is meant to be traveled and enjoyed."
—Unknown

Well, folks, thanks for stopping by, and I'll see you on the road.

CHAPTER 22

Minnesota: One State
Away from Home

April 2021

Our very last camping spot before ending our journey would be in a gorgeous area in southeast Minnesota called Isinours Management Area. This campground (which, of course, is free!) is outside the quaint little town of Lanesboro, Minnesota, in the Richard J. Dorer Memorial Hardwood State Forest, run by the state DNR. The campsites are primitive and are situated along the Root River Trail—an excellent paved trail for hiking and biking. The town of Lanesboro has a population of less than eight hundred, and I think it is the prettiest town I have ever seen! The Root River flows through town, and there is even a picturesque waterfall along the river and bike trail. This little town was also given the title of one of the "20 best dream towns in America" by *Outside* magazine.

The weather was decent with sunny sixties by day and almost forty degrees by night, so we enjoyed two nights at this beautiful spot including a couple of trips to town to walk the trail and take pictures of the river and waterfall.

On April 18, almost five months after starting this journey of a lifetime (which I intend to continue!), we departed Lanesboro, Minnesota, for a slow and off-the-beaten-path return trip home to Luck, Wisconsin. Seeing the green grass and yellow daffodils along with familiar sights of dairy farms, horses, and green pastureland was very comforting. I was torn between the familiarity of my home state of Wisconsin and the memories of places and people that would be no longer in my life. As we passed the places closer to home, memories of the days with my mom came flooding back and opened up the floodgates of my tears.

> "Heavy hearts, like heavy clouds in the sky are best relieved by the letting of a little water."
> —Christopher Morley

I hadn't cried recently as our travels seemed to keep the sadness and emptiness at bay. But knowing that my mom had taken the most beautiful and important journey of her lifetime and that she is now hanging out with Jesus, nothing else could be as comforting. And knowing that someday I will take that all-important journey too is, without a doubt, the very most comforting feeling in the world.

Thanks for stopping by, and I'll see you on the road.

Waterfalls in Lanesboro, Minnesota

CHAPTER 23

Welcome Home: Getting Back to the "New Normal"

April 2021

Well, we had been on the road on the journey of a lifetime for five months. For over one hundred and fifty days, we had lived (except for 2 days) without electricity, without heat, and without running water or a toilet (except for an occasional porta-potty!). We had boondocked in the desert and the mountains on free public land or dispersed national forest camping areas. We had soaked in the sun by day and the campfire by night. Endless days were spent outside in the wide-open spaces in the wild blue yonder, watching birds and wildlife. Nights were filled with stargazing and moon-searching, listening to a hooting owl or a howling coyote. Nothing can fill you with peace and tranquility like being one with nature and being in total awe and amazement of God's creation.

I truly believe that taking this trip was the very best thing I could have done after my mom died. To have unlimited time to remember her, to reflect on our lives together and to mourn the fact that she is gone. There was an ever-present feeling that God has been with me on this entire journey, and I have faith in knowing that He was also definitely with her when she took her last breath. I still feel connected to her even though we are physically apart, knowing that our love will continue to be there forever. Those are the thoughts that heal the heart and bring peace to the soul.

"The best remedy for those who are afraid, lonely or unhappy is to go outside, somewhere where they can be quiet, alone with the heavens, nature and God. Because only then does one feel that all is as it should be and that God wishes to see people happy, amidst the simple beauty of nature."
—Anne Frank

I am so thankful that my husband and I are old enough to be retired but still young and healthy enough to take these adventures. Knowing that we can take as much time or as little time as we want in each location. Never having to worry about all the rules and regulations, not to mention the reservations that almost all of the RV parks and organized campgrounds require. Being out on the open highway and the backroads of America, looking for the next awesome place to stay and explore. That is the very best part of the joy and excitement of the journey. Being what I like to call a "free agent," which basically means that we are not obligated to any person, place or time. Total freedom! I love it, and I want more!

Coming back to our home in Wisconsin and the reality of all the responsibilities of being a homeowner was a rude awakening. Leaves needed to be raked, the grass needed to be mowed, the house needed to be cleaned, the windows needed to be washed...the list goes on and on. Being in our little Easy Breezy camper for all those months seemed so easy and simple, hence the name Easy Breezy! You take care of your camper and your tow vehicle when it needs something, but other than that, it seems as if there is very little maintenance and work required. And when you're living on the road, you have the luxury of having a lot of time on your hands. There's an occasional amount of upkeep, no yard work, no projects, and no time-wasting distractions like television. Just you and the out-of-doors soaking in the beauty of it all. That, to me, is the very best way to spend the day.

I will always be grateful to God for the abilities and freedoms that He has given me. Knowing that He has been there with me throughout this adventure brings me boatloads of joy and peace.

There is no better feeling in the universe than knowing that our Father in heaven is everywhere you are.

Thank you for coming along on the ride. It's been a pleasure to bring you along!

CHAPTER 24

A Crappy Welcome-Home Gift

May 2021

Well, the title of the last chapter was a bit of a misnomer. Getting back to the "new normal"—not quite yet! Unfortunately, there was an unwelcome homecoming gift waiting for me four days after we returned…Covid! I know. Can you believe it? After five months of living remotely in the desert, I got it from pretty much the very first person I was with (a friend of mine who was unaware that she had it!) And *wham*, three days later, I got sick.

I knew on the second day that this was something that I never had before, and we had plans to celebrate my husband's mom's ninety-third birthday with her. So I called to get tested. I made the phone call at 8:00 AM and got tested that day at 10:30 AM. I received a call with the results about 24 hours later, and the results were positive. I had Covid!

I couldn't believe it! I had worked really hard to make sure my husband and I were safe; we wore a mask any time we went to a store or gas station and had hand sanitizer everywhere.

So yeah, Covid is no fun. It is definitely not something you want to mess with, and I consider myself fairly healthy! I am now currently on day 11 and am still not feeling well. I have a fever, body aches, tension headache, and no sense of smell or taste, and the worst of all is the brain fog and having absolutely zero energy! I do not like being sick, but I especially hate not having any energy. Luckily, my husband doesn't seem to be experiencing any symptoms, so maybe he will defy the odds and not get it.

I have also been feeling extra emotional these days as May 2 was my mom's first birthday in heaven, and of course, next Sunday is my first Mother's Day without her in sixty-three years. It also would have been my parent's sixty-eighth wedding anniversary as they were married on May 9, 1953. So yes, May has been a sad month for me, and I have been missing my mom and also my dad (who has been gone for almost seven years). I feel blessed to have had my mom for sixty-two years, but that still doesn't make the fact that she is no longer with me any less painful.

My prayer for Mother's Day this year would be that all of you out there who are blessed to still have your moms will feel extra appreciation for them not just on Mother's Day but every single day. Why wait for only one day in a whole year to let your mom know how special she is and how much you love her? Do it every day!

"All that I am, or ever hope to be, I owe to my angel mother."
—Abraham Lincoln

Mom on Mother's Day

CHAPTER 25

Until We Meet Again

"Nobody can go back and start a new beginning,
but anyone can start today and make a new
ending."
—Maria Robinson

May 2021

Well, folks, this is it. The final chapter. At least of this journey!

As I said in a previous chapter, this was the trip of a lifetime, and I plan on continuing the journey as soon as possible. The plans are in the works to sell our home and almost all our earthly possessions this summer and get back out there.

My desire to become a full-time nomad has only grown stronger now that I have five months under my belt. I'm not saying I will never again be a homeowner, but what I am saying is that this newfound freedom of the open highway has really gotten under my skin. I have fallen in love with this lifestyle, and I am hooked! To see this entire beautiful country of ours one back road at a time could take years, and that is exactly what my plan is—at least while we are still young and healthy enough to enjoy it. Life is short, and the clock is ticking! My plan is to quit wasting the pretty, get back out in that wild blue yonder, and explore! To see beautiful sights and meet interesting folks along the way. To see God's unending beauty up-close and personal every single day for the rest of our time on this earth.

> "When I'm old and dying, I plan to look back on
> my life and say, "Wow, that was an adventure,"
> not, "Wow, I sure felt safe.""
>
> —Tom Preston-Werner

And, when our life is over, knowing that our ultimate journey is yet to come. I thank the Lord that every day until then I have the privilege and the freedom to explore this glorious planet and bask in the awesomeness of His creation.

That is my wish for all of you too.

In the words of Roy Rogers and Dale Evans,

> Happy trails to you,
> Until we meet again.
> Happy trails to you,
> Keep smiling until then.

Thanks for coming along on the journey, and I can't wait to see you on the road!

> "The biggest adventure you can ever take is to
> live the life of your dreams."
>
> —Oprah Winfrey

Me and my husband, Jeff

Raven Rae—Age 13

Rocky Rocco—Age 16 ½!

About the Author

Shari Lee Fleming is a self-professed gypsy who was born with a calling and a passion to wander. She has lived and worked in six different states in her lifetime before recently retiring. After writing this book, she has been fortunate enough to become a full-time nomad. She is currently "happily houseless" and fulfilling her dream of living on the road in a twenty-five-foot travel trailer, appropriately called The Lollygagger, with her husband Jeff and her two canine companions—Rocky and Raven.

Her goal is to travel this great country, basking in God's beauty and sharing her faith and love of travel with others along the way.

"I'll see you on the road!"

CPSIA information can be obtained
at www.ICGtesting.com
Printed in the USA
LVHW071148261022
731595LV00010B/214